CW01304221

these things i carry

poems by theresa wu

a journey through postpartum depression

Ko Wan Creative Edition 2024

Copyright © 2024 by Ko Wan Creative

All rights reserved. No part of this publication may be reproduced, stored or transmitted, in any form or by any means, without prior permission with Ko Wan Creative.

For information about permission to reproduce selections from this book, write to info@kowancreative.com

Visit the website www.kowancreative.com for more information about this book or the author.

Printed in the United States of America.

Dedicated to Alexander.
May you overcome the storms that blindside you.
Let it lift you, toss you about,
and help you reckon with the darkness
so that you can find the light that was always within,
always there,
and that is forever yours.

table of contents

foreword	8
100 words	14
fingerprints	18
steam rises	26
fireworks	38
car ride home	46
wednesday night	52
dear friend	58
third goodbye	62
the first light	68
gone with the wind	74
déjà vu	96
knockout	102
roulette	108
we went to the mountains	112
it all went fine	126
birth marks	136
emancipation	142
these things i carry	148
afterword	156

FOREWORD

It took me five years to write this. To find my way back to the mainland. To find my voice, I thought was destroyed. To understand that all this darkness was to help me find a light, that I thought I had to earn.

I never intended to share my journey through Postpartum Depression (PPD) with anyone. The journey was to hide within the four walls of my home until it was over. And the really bad parts, in the four walls of my mind. But what I thought was to be six months at most, lasted two and a half years. It was the hardest time in my life. I felt the weight of death follow me everywhere I went, knowing I could drown at any given moment. Meanwhile, there was this amazing and beautiful life I felt nothing towards. All emotions were on mute and I had no power to move the needle on any of it. I could not give or receive the warmth, love or care that I assumed was every mother's birthright. As a sensitive and emotional soul, I was completely lost without my superpower to feel. Without my ground. Without my mind. It took everything inside of me to wake up each day and not want to walk directly into the ocean.

I was told that persons predisposed to depression and those who experienced trauma, were more likely to get PPD. It was described to me as the blues due to fatigue and lack of self-care. I didn't think I would get it. My traumas and depressions were long sorted out with therapy years past and my self-care was already engaged. Like most illnesses, there are varying degrees of PPD. Like most births, there are varying degrees of trauma. Physical will always be talked about, but the mental and emotional toll of a difficult birth was glossed over in all the baby books, and was not addressed in the hospital or care afterwards. Surely, I was not alone in my experience in all the years of motherhood and all the mothers in the world. Where were all the tools, support and methods for managing, caring and treating this condition?

To this day, I have received many conflicting opinions from many doctors and therapists on what is PPD, how long it lasts, how to treat it and if it can come back. My first episode of PPD lasted one and a half year until I stopped breastfeeding. But then, two months later, returned with a vengeance when I tried a non-hormonal IUD. Ultimately, medication was not for me and so I braced myself for the dark unknown. With physical therapy for physical ailments, talk therapy for my mind and the bravery of my husband to show up everyday looking for me, even though I was lost at sea, I got through those difficult, almost tragic, years. Three years ago, I wrote my obituary with the clear acceptance that I was going to loose this battle. But through the grace of God and a miracle, I found my way home.

There are many horrible experiences that I can't write about in specific memoir detail about the birth of my child. But this book isn't about that day, but days and moments after. I had a very traumatizing birth and experienced many failures that day which contributed and set off a very debilitating time in my life. This is a story about that mountain and the self I had pieced back together after the storm of my lifetime blew through and wiped out everything I trusted was going to be there when I returned. My sanity and marriage were tried and tested. Both, barely survived.

What was to be one of the most brilliant experiences of my life, was one of my darkest. My recovery took years and I am only now beginning to process all that I have been through in the past five years. I start from this moment. A chapter I did not imagine; a chapter not yet written in the stars. I start as a mother and a survivor of the most beautiful and devastating time in my life.

This book is my first step back.

Postpartum Depression is chemical, emotional, hormonal, and different for each who suffers from it. This is my experience.

Thank you for reading. Thank you for bearing witness.

Theresa

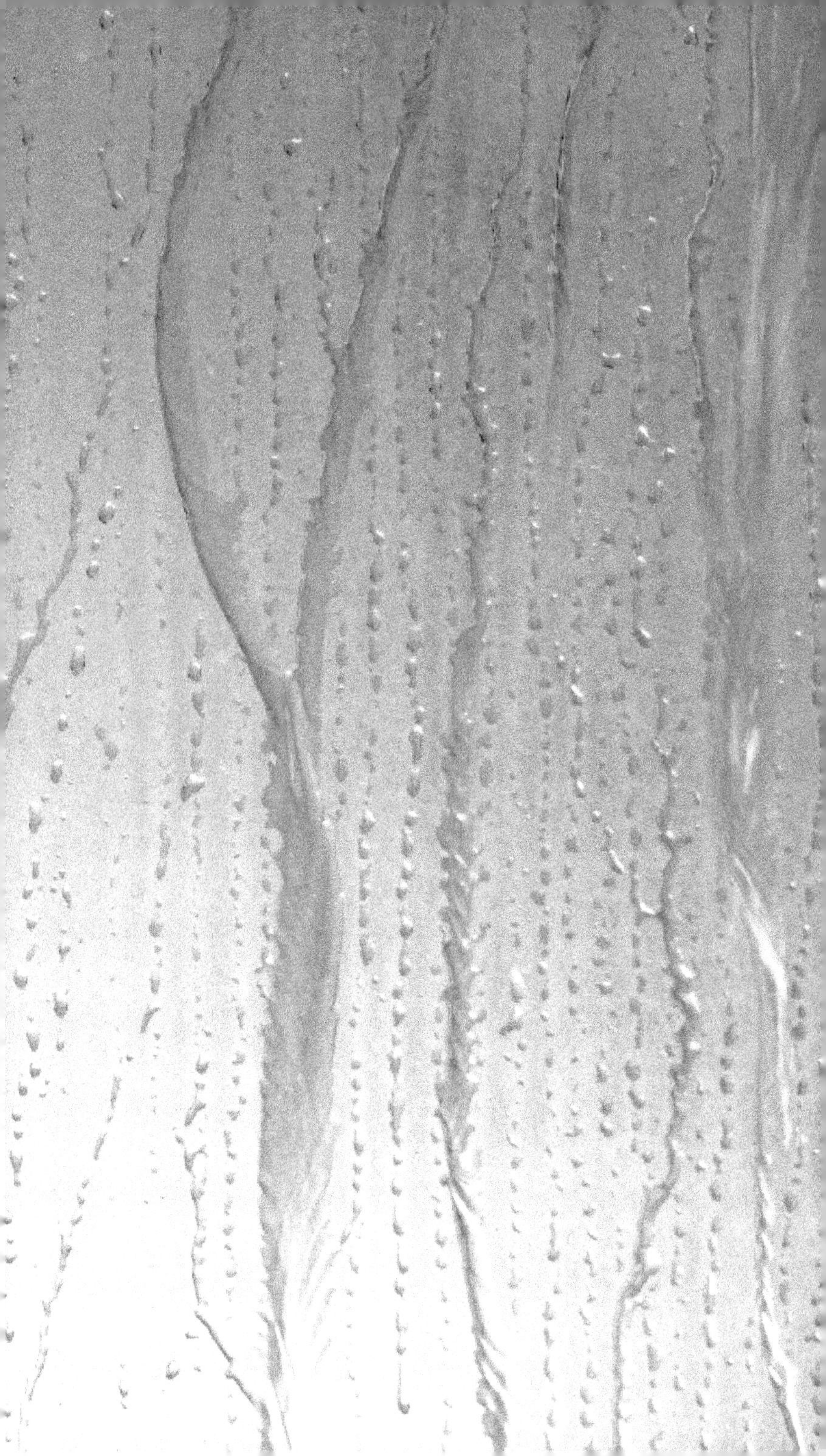

100 words

*A rejected entry for the 2019 Christmas edition of
Modern Love in the NY Times.*

we started in september.
chances, slim.
your eggs are dying, she said.
i know.
he tested. turns out, he would discover the same sadness.
but we tried anyway. peed on sticks. timed out kisses.
organic. no chips. we cheered. hoped. cried.
and mourned. twice. it could still happen.
try. again. again. and again.
then the doctor confirmed it.
there's no chance, i'm so sorry.
my heart sunk. drove home, sobbing.
let it go.
this wasn't yours. it isn't yours.
eyes red, but he didn't cry. silence. then he said, let's kiss.
why? it's over.
for us, he said.
so we kissed.
nine months later on christmas day
our son was born.

fingerprints

i can't remember
what it was like

memories borrowed from photographs
filled in by imagination
about moments
i will never recall

unable to forget
that which has been seared into my dna
i play on repeat wondering
when i could have done something, anything
to prevent
the
trauma

they don't tell you about this part
the invisible scars that will
mark all your memories
the nurse who did not make conversation
the wordless gesture
of emptying my bladder
into a bag, removed too soon
discharged before i could walk again
what if the feeling
in my leg
never comes back?
what if my continence
never comes back?
what if my feelings
never come
back?

how will i love you?

hollow
parts of me have been removed
ransacked
i didn't know
i didn't build anything
of permanence
i didn't know
i was
empty
i didn't know
you
gave me
worth
which means
everything else
had given
nothing

i didn't think
it would be so hard
that the love i once felt
was always just a shadow
a figment of an overactive imagination
now looking at it's reflection
it's not that i want to die
i just don't want to live
my days, a broken record
unconnected
to the reasons
why

spinning in circles
trying to keep from drowning
every hour
on the hour
i'm exhausted
and no one can save me
no one
can respond
in kind

the inability
to feel
to go through the emotions
and no power
to experience them
i would cry
he would beg
i don't know what to say to him
i don't know how to tell him how to help
i am stuck on an island
and he was on the mainland
with you
and i am over here
surrounded by
the inability
to swim
how can i explain this?
how can he save me?
if i cant,
i believe
it's easier
if

i am not saved

everyday
i would feel one thing
the constant
relentless, in this rip tide:
i could give all this up
any moment
if asked
any moment
if presented
any moment
i could fall
between the cracks
if i held my breath too long
if i closed my eyes for one more second
if i let go
of the idea that i would ever
return
but in pieces

i am falling
each day
the tide takes me
the shadows magnify
the original reasons
become irrelevant
i can't hear you
i can't see you
i can't

i've always existed alone

even with him
comfortable without anyone
accepting that there was no one
who wanted
to share my space
yet there exists a barrenness to my existence
a fragility i hadn't noticed until
now
a silence that burns
a vision so bright
my eyes are best closed
no one can know
i am seconds away
to walking into
the waters
just as
i am
or once
was

so collect
bear witness
so someone will be able to tell you
all the things
i can't remember

and mindful to,
never
share
all the things
i do.

steam rises

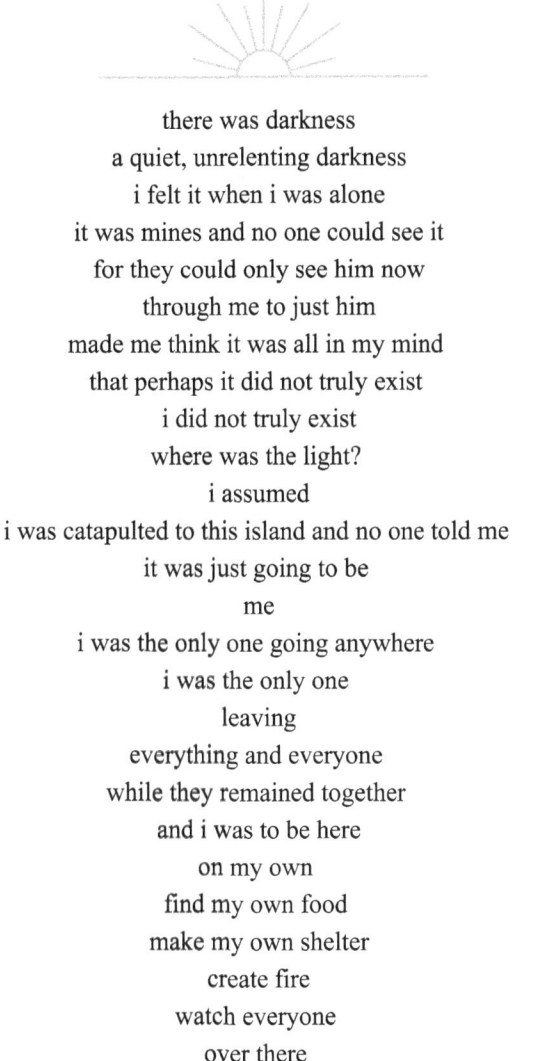

there was darkness
a quiet, unrelenting darkness
i felt it when i was alone
it was mines and no one could see it
for they could only see him now
through me to just him
made me think it was all in my mind
that perhaps it did not truly exist
i did not truly exist
where was the light?
i assumed
i was catapulted to this island and no one told me
it was just going to be

me

i was the only one going anywhere
i was the only one
leaving
everything and everyone
while they remained together
and i was to be here
on my own
find my own food
make my own shelter
create fire
watch everyone
over there
in all their
joy

sit. just sit.

he tells me to take my time. to yell if i need help.
i just want to be alone.
you don't have to be, he replies.
i want to do this myself.
but i can help you, he pleads.

no you can't. no one can help me.

i take a breath and start again.
i need this. i can do nothing myself. let me do this.
a bloated pause.
he relents knowing he is no match for my new title.
i can hear his fading footsteps.

sit. just sit.

there were handles on both sides so i didn't fall.
it barely fit.
my mother measured the whole tub
instead of just the opening.
i can't get mad at her i tell myself.
she meant well.

i turn on the water. i feel the temperature.
hot. like i like it.
scalding.
i remember being ten, standing in my childhood shower,
mom screaming at the door
WHY ARE YOU TAKING SO LONG?
WATER COSTS MONEY.

YOU'RE CLEAN.
COME OUT.
i stood with my head against the hard tile in our 3x3 shower
eyes closed.
wash me away, i prayed.
help me disappear.

i open the sliding door and lock my knee.
keep it locked, i remind myself in a scolding tone.
don't fall.
if you fall, the water will drown you.
lock it. lock it dammit. if you don't…
three. two. one.
i'm in.

sit. just sit.

the hot water rushes down my back. coats my head.
runs down my face
and my tears. they fuse with the water
off my eyelashes
off the tip of my nose
around my shoulders
like rain without relief

steam begins to rise

i close my eyes.
wash me.
wash me away.
help me.
help me disappear.

help me to...

are you okay? he interrupts.
i'm fine!!
he leaves again.
i didn't mean to yell.

sit. just sit.

i shiver.
i try to turn around to face the water but i can't
i am stuck
the chair is in the way
i'm freezing now
i try again
inches away and i can't reach
paralyzed further than my leg
i should sit
i should

maybe if i stay standing?
who do you think you are?
i won't fall.
you will. you won't get up.
you will drown.
what will he do without you?
what will the boy do?
without.
you don't get this.
no one can be without you.
don't move. you need what you didn't expect.
everything is on purpose.

and besides,
you will loose.

a stubborn fool, i try once more
i reach further
than i could
than i should
than i can
and tears flow immediately
fuck
i turn back to face the white tiles
three inches
ricochet back
on my
eyelids

so i sit.
finally.

the hot water rushes on my back. coats my head.
runs down my face
and my tears
i try to catch them. one by one. i try.
but i can't
they're coming so fast. there's too many. stop.
i just need a moment. stop.
give. me. a. moment.
stop,
i beg.
gasping,
my palms touch my face. encapsulates it.
there

i hold steady as they fill my hands
don't move.
if i don't move, they won't fall
i won't fall.
i won't even notice
that
i
can't
breathe

sit. just sit.

i am looking
does someone have me?
does someone have this?
why is it so dark?
i am looking
for
someone

tears splash on my thighs, sitting on the cold plastic seat
i see a blue rectangle sky
it's so clear outside
but i don't see anyone
or anything
behind the steam,
i know no one
can
see
me

my head hangs back down

towards my scar
the incision unevenly threaded through my skin
the sharp edges of the thread
prick me
reminds me
with my wrinkled fingers i feel it
all the parts i can't feel,
places i once felt
so much

footsteps

he didn't stop
he didn't exhale
he was hoping
pretending
i was okay
that nothing
happened
i hold my breath
and listen
but he's already gone
he doesn't know
i don't know
i need him

don't let them down
stay seated
take your place
it happened
this is where you are now

with a hole in the center of my body
in the middle of my soul
caught in my throat
stealing my voice
my words
lost in
the experience
riddled with empty pockets
of
darkness
so my grasp always comes up
bloodied
with chunks
fragments
i lost
along the way
forgetful
to remind myself
to leave
breadcrumbs

so sit
just sit
and let the steam rise...

...i look downward to see
the bathtub is the shape of a coffin
such a small space
to rest forever in.

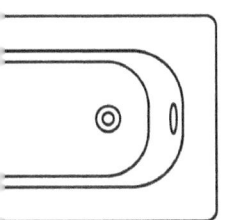

fireworks

ready. get set. GO.

bombs are going off inside of me
in sequence
to an invisible
chorus of violins
a long awaited symphony
one by one
i feel the ground tremble
and jump ever so slight
at each explosion
of thought

they all cheer
as if their experience was a fifth of my own
but i cower
afraid of the pauses
afraid of where
all those fireworks
will land
terror seizes my
breath

he wants to fix something he can't see
he wants to help me see things from a different perspective
he wants to visit me, when i am stuck on an island,
even god can't reach
he wants so much
at a time, i am at a loss
unable to even give myself
a moment to grieve
so that i can

wash
away
this new stain
after i had just gotten rid of
the heartache
of not being good enough

rush
hurry up
focus
stay the course
he needs you
he is paying so much for your lack
and they're all afraid looking sideways
smiling cautiously
avoiding asking
how are you?
what are you doing?
how are you feeling?
shouldn't you medicate?
they're all afraid
of you
of what you are capable of
of what you will make
of this
of what
you
will
destroy

don't wallow
don't grieve

time is elusive
and it is saved for someone else
deserving

didn't they tell you?
didn't anyone warn?
well, you should have known
it was never going to circle back
it was never
about
you

all those shadows
demons lying in wait
this lesson
this horror
this lack
you need
to survive the depths
the scarcity

i have no answers for him
i can't even tell him
what i want to eat
all i know is that i'm
starving
i can't even tell him
why
i don't care
when i'm cradling you
in my hands
your tiny fingers

over
my
pulse

you hold me
you trust
you want to know
why
i stare off in the distance
a sadness washes over my despondent smile
you want to know
why
you are watching
waiting
for me
to appear

why

i'm in the forest again
without him
without
everything that has led me forward
without you
without

so here is the key
the price
your only breath

shave off a minute here
a minute there

a few more minutes
and then it will all fit
and then
you can be who you need to be
for him
for them
eat a little faster
sleep a little less
don't
worry about
what you look like
because what you feel like
will
always
reign

give it up
let go
be this
be who you are
less than you hoped
more than you feared

this way
this way through the forest
so get back on your hands and knees
find the ground
so you can find your way through
so you can
find
a spot in the darkness
where no one can see you

where you can pretend
all this
was
on
purpose

frantic, i wave
but alas, no one can see past you
no one can see me
no one can see
that i am disappearing
into
that
forest
fading into the green
packed down in the brown
and buried.

car ride home

it's cold
i'm always cold
he thought i needed air
but i don't
he assumed it would be warmer
but he forgets
i am not him
and he has no idea
but he wants to
his earnest desire to feel
what i feel
and understand
the lack of feeling
for a part of me i created

there is a sadness to my everyday
my tears are dry
my joy painted on
i wake at 5 to put on my face
so i won't look
like i don't care
so i won't look
how i feel
you'll see my smile
feel my hugs
share in the laughter
but i cannot dare show you
my state of rest
my state

i am broken
torn apart

sewn, not quite enough
regretful
of all that i left behind
of all i did not finish
did i give up?
or was i never good enough?
does it matter
that i won that award
that even strangers gasp at
or that i wanted to change the world
by healing
that child
who didn't have enough
convinced she wasn't enough
does it matter
that i chose, not knowing i was choosing between
does any of it matter
when i am 90
will i have lived a life worth living
or will i have regretted not living
not doing
what i told myself
i was capable of
and still
am

i hope

that despite
the silence
within this captivity
that you

are my north star
you
are light infinite
and it is you,
my soul
chose

will you forgive me
someday
will you shine
even though
there was no light
will you remember
my love,
when i slipped,
and couldn't find my footing
how long
will you mistake this darkness
for your own?
will you remember?

and yet
i am certain
you are perfect
and through that i see, now
there was never anything wrong with me

i
too
had,
have
light

and if i could just feel that
if i could
maybe
i would want to stay
i would want to fight
i would forgive the desire to
end this
every
day

imagine
i would
know
my north star
where you are
who you are
and how to get home

so just drive
he doesn't want to know
he doesn't want to feel
he will not want
this
he does not want
this

i am cold
and i will adjust.

wednesday night

my eyes burn
and i am back, turned around
i can't look at him no more
shelling out apologies as if one meant more than the other

no one asked him to fix
the thing he did not break
no one asked him to tell me
how to do this better
his arrogance
steals all the oxygen
so deafening
he doesn't even hear me
walk away

so go sit and sulk
he deserves where he is at
my empathy is saved for
someone who has not shown up yet
who promised
was already here

part of me wants to step away
i want to go under and never
come up for air
but i know
that this is bigger than him
everything is bigger than him
bigger than me
he thinks i gave him that much power
power given to himself, by himself
in reality

i gave it to much less deserving people

so for now
i just want to sleep alone
his desperation
to be forgiven
his pleas to be heard
forgive yourself
hear yourself
then you won't have to wonder
why i left

everything about it
i don't want
we outgrew it years past
like an echo
words, familiar
as if
we had only passed this once
as if he lied to himself
that day he stood before me
convinced if he just showed up
he'd
overflow

he promised what he didn't know
he wasn't capable of

i thought,
but now i know
he does the best he can

that little boy
who was never told how to be kind
was never taught
to be kind
who was never told
why
that his cluelessness
was funny
almost charming
he thought his privilege
was enough to sustain
his least finest tool,
a secret i discovered
last

i will not
stoop down
bend down
reach down
to get
to where he is at
where he chooses to be
where he claims he is not
to be
with him
to feel
his love
to do this on a Wednesday

so
leave me the fuck alone
the conversation has ended.

dear friend

i wade in the deep end
you think this is joy
but this is two seconds away
from
drowning
you see only water
pristine
reflecting light
you don't notice
the darkness
the depths
the undertow
and my feet
unable to tread
touch the bottom
unable to remember
how to save myself
why

and silence is what you offered
as if i am better alone
than i am with a response
something
anything
to tell me
i wasn't alone

shame on you

where do i put you
do i let you leave with everyone else
do i send you away

when you didn't show up
it's not personal
i convince myself
you have no idea the depths of these oceans
if you've never left the shore

so i sit here
and wrestle with the dark shadows
that mimic my own
i can't seem
to turn my head
turn the page
captive to a chapter
i closed a long time ago
and yet, there was always room for its return
so perhaps this is mines
all mines
it was just time
to go to the depths
and wade
in the waters that could drown me

shame on me
for waiting
for you.

the first light

In the midst of my PPD, my husband went into heart failure. I stopped breastfeeding in preparation. This was his third open heart surgery. A week hospital stay turned into two when a complication arose and he unexpectantly went into his fourth. The PPD was overshadowed by the one storm, greater than mines.

we arrived early
sun tucked away behind shadows of slate skies
palm trees lead us through echoing streets
so we could walk
hand in hand
wordless
in no rush to make the green light
like when we were younger
when these steps
could fill me up for weeks

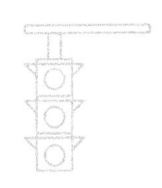

and now i try and memorize
where he lays his fingers on mines
his mindful cradle of my hand,
even when his attention holds its breath
its been so long
since so much
how did we forget
so fast
so easily
regretfully
we try and soak up the minutes like the hours we wasted
i try to match his steps
but our strides differ
i've always known
but today,
i try
anyway

i remember last time
watching our reflection in the subway cart
i sat next to him, empty seats scattered

clear view of his sorrow
surprised how a reflection
could be filled with such precision of what we hide
for everyone to see
and yet, no one is watching
even me
i watch myself, disappointed
i am waiting
anticipating
drowning in the story i've created,
so i can blunt the sword
if it comes
when it comes
as it comes
the subway lurches forward and my gaze steadies
i am reminded
i may never arrive
i take this moment to wallow in my own grief
shallow in comparison to his
the sound of the doors, lift both our gazes
snaps us out of this indulgent moment
as we get off as silently as we sat
leaving our broken selves in that reflection,
knowing which steps to take
to return us
home

but this time,
in the still of the dawn
i think of how many times i will think
of this walk
my bags packed, in case

his bags empty, in case
feeling it is almost time
despite how early
we
showed
up

as we head up the final hill
ready?
he replies with a smile
a knowing, i wish wasn't his
we exchange words
etched in our silences
lets take a moment, i finally say
he pauses to rest on a divider, set at the exact height
his racing heart throbs, struggles
as his hand smooths the hair from my tears
i lean into his warm palm
he asks
i falter
and embrace him
we stand frozen
together
but apart

i can see in my mind
as if i was across the street
watching a couple in front of a hospital
wondering what loss they just had
or what loss
is about to ensue
creating a story

a painting
so
i'll always
remember
what it felt like
the moments before

the doors slide open behind us
we both turn and look
no one enters
no one exits

we should go, he urges
he should
i should
we know
it is the only path
that leads us
somewhere else
besides here

early
but on time
in sickness and in health
in death do us part.

third goodbye

we face the gauntlet again
this time assured by the experience but no less
frightened by the knowledge
that any day, this day
could be your last

how did we get here so soon
to weave through the emotions of waiting
of wondering
of being present for the sheer knowing
we may pass through this just
once more

and yet,
my flaws proliferate
my voice raises at things
that you swear you didn't mean
and i get upset
knowing you are doing only your best
just killing time
as we wait
for
the day

the chilly air rushes in the small window
i secretly enjoy
as our heat is higher than we can afford
to comfort our son during his illness
but this chill
a luxury,
alone in my office
pretending i had no where to go

do
or become

what do i care now
i am here
no one is waiting
or anticipating
magic hour has passed
and i've become faint
finally alone, i can't even reach
for something
i once knew so well
to help me patch together
into some poetic tale
voice turned to stone
words turned to ash
years of stories,
i cringe at the childlike perspective
innocent but limited
wondrous, but foolish
it has become a relic within
i hold onto
when so much awaits me here
at each sunrise
to let go of

if i could only arrive
if i could only be here now
if only
before it all passes and disappears into a memory
that i won't have
when all this is over

i can't ask him to remember
for me
he can't see
fact is
he is just as powerless as i am
he has no vision
and i no longer can see mines
he has no instinct
and i can no longer feel mines
turns out
at the end of the day
i am like everyone else
guilty of the same shit
blind
trying to find a way
trying to find hope
trying to keep from crying in front of the other

trying to believe
one of us won't die
first

it's a different number
but the same waiting room
the same visitor's badge
the same elevator
the same goodbye

you got this
i love you
i will see you when you wake up

and he holds onto my words, more than he did last time
i try to remember his warmth
as strangers in matching outfits
watch me
waiting for me to finish

and so it is done
our goodbyes
have
been
said.

gone with the wind

The following September my PPD was suddenly gone.
Instantly, I could feel the sun again. I could feel my son.

As my husband healed, so did I.

and then it was gone

what was to be weeks
was months
two Christmases
i missed
encompassed by forces
settled into
the dark spot in my brain
i now
can never get rid of
and the fear, the knowledge
i can never
reclaim
that space
again

it had made itself known
hollered
clawed
echoed
in all my waking moments
and then
my god
it left
i can't tell you how
i can't tell you when
i can tell you,
as i stepped away
and came back
the walls weren't
there

the tower
wasn't real
i was on ground
back in my house
on the mainland
as if i never left
even though i knew
i was gone
by the layer of dust
collected
kept warm
in the effervescent sunlight
i missed
each sunset

but also
the memories
i can't recall
i can't seem to feel
what i see in the photos
like a tunnel
dark and silent
but when its over
light
        light
                light
one can't recall
the dream
and i look at the images
to trigger the happiness i see in your face
but i am miming in
a black hole

and i see
and i know
i
wasn't
there

shame fills my goosebumps
as i think to myself
thank god
people only need a photo
if only
i did too
i don't know those moments
i don't know who you were
but i know who i was
a ghost
pretending
to feel
what it was like
to be with you
and when i go to the ocean's edge
to feel the light
that now warms my skin
i see
the sticks that scraped my hands
my back
my arches
the blanket of dried seaweed
that flew off in the wind
and scattered
the sand like confetti
permeating every crevice

of my eyes
remnants of myself
discarded, torn, thrown about
littered like seashells thrown on shore
from the ocean's waves
as if i had been swallowed
whole
and had disappeared under the current
and then
spat back out

i was
in pieces
separated at birth
with no power
to arrive
stagnant, as the world continued to dance
i won't lie
i can't forget
but
i pray to

my face has aged
belly soft
my eyes shifts downward
dark spots litter my face like in my mind
my body broken
into
scars
like tattoos i misjudged
of what now has become
phantom pain

eighteen months later
your arm drapes on me
as you fall asleep
refusing your crib for hours
days
your small voice calls out
mama
        mama
                mama
as i sneak into the bathroom
to put on the eyebrows
that make me feel
less missing
you shimmy a dance in your seat
as i give you a homemade muffin
to be the mom, i always wanted
to be the mom, i am not capable of becoming
your eyes light up
excited for the full sugar content
smushed in your whole fist
raspberry on your nose
you smile
and look at me
the way my husband has always looked at me
with complete and utter
love

you, like him,
are taken
by my empty gestures to fulfill my younger self
ignored and malnourished
broken open by sadness

but also
the adult self
locked in by the past
that won't forgive
herself
for not becoming better
or more

so
what is so obvious now
that was elusive before
is now there are
two
two people
who
want to hold my heart
and want me
to hold
theirs

the audacity
the absurdness
the privilege

i can't tell anyone what it was
i can only say
it was silent
hollow
lonely
like a storm
that wouldn't let up
rain

for a year and a half
always soaked
always trying to find shelter
surviving
the cuts
the bites
the nightmares
the rip tides
while being held ransom
for all that you won't do
won't eat
won't say
you
who will never know
my smile was painted
my laughter feigned
my excitement copied
my presence
absent
knowing
i will take nothing with me
of these experiences
i will get nothing
with you
only pictures i can't remember

until now

it is gone
i have materialized
i am here
i lean into you

pretending to enjoy the fire trucks running over my scars
as your eyes cast over towards me
looking
searching
you catch my gaze and i am caught off guard
you love
like your father
you smile
like me

then i see
you see me

what if
in fact

you always had.

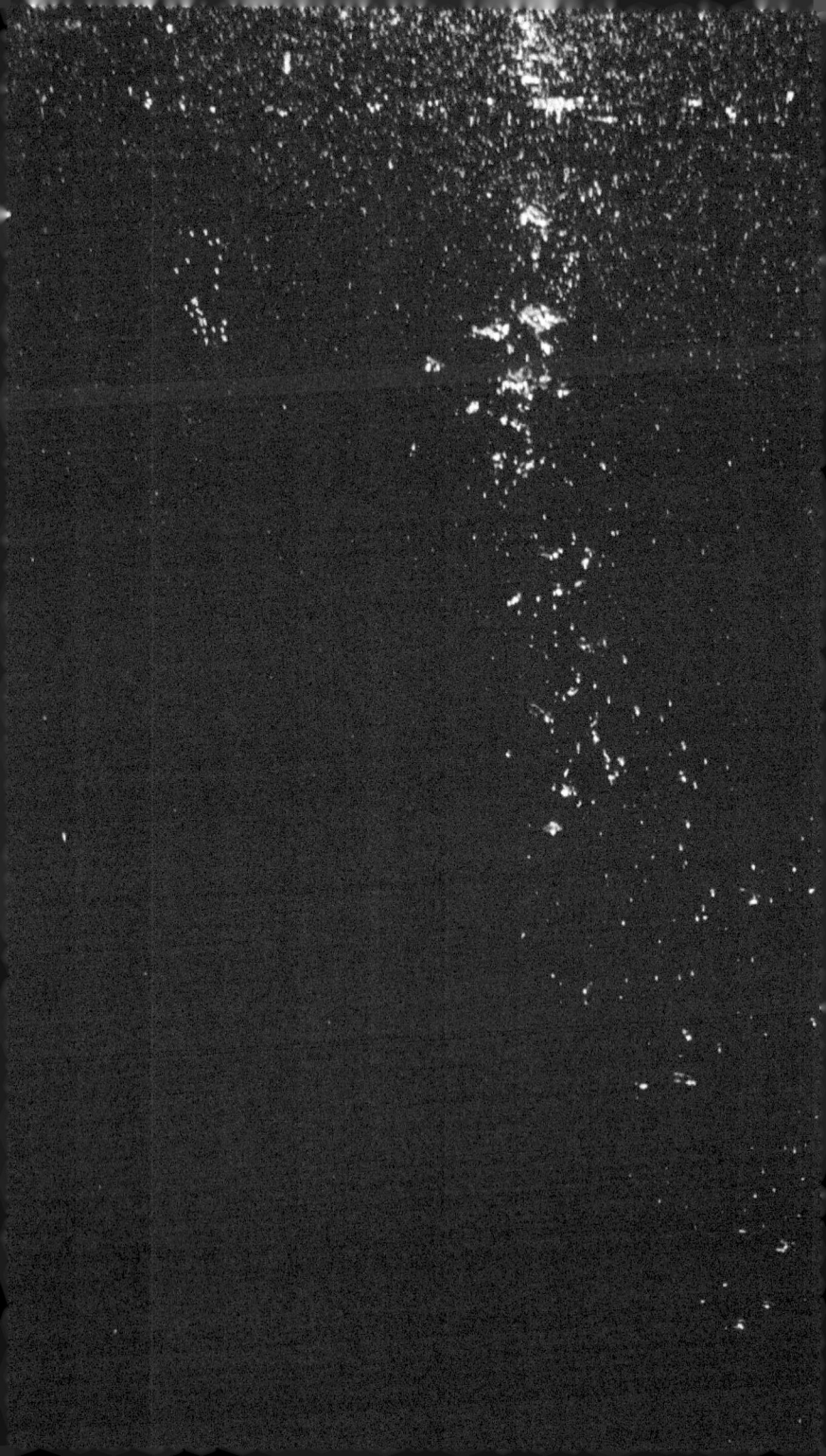

from the corner i see you
but i cannot come
in the corner
around a wall
you cannot see me
you cannot reach me
no one can
tears soak my shirt
i should have thrown out years ago
pilled and stained
i wear
to hide the uglier stain
underneath
you call for me
and i rush to catch my breath
i rush
to stuff it all back it
to make sure
nothing leaks out
onto you

the sound of the food processor rumbles
as my mind filters out
everything necessary
but blank spaces
as someone like me
without someone like you
receives
something i do not deserve
but use to think
believe
hope
i could
my hair uncombed for days
pressing hard
to continue eviscerating
drowning out the audience cheering
to hide my disappointment
dripping into
the homemade chicken nuggets
i was convinced to make
to mold you into
at least
a better human
than i am
i close my eyes
and wait
it is almost over

i hide
when i can
he closes his eyes
when he sees me
when he looks for me
i close mines
behind my walls
there are no windows
no door
no one will notice
if i find
the only exit

wash me away
help me to disappear

déjà vu

After two months the PPD returned,
worst than before.

and then it came back with a vengeance
without warning, i chose by ignorance
and i am further back than the darkest day
its not that i wanted to die
it was inevitable
this was going to
end me

i had dreams of someone i once loved
who i don't trust
to remember me with any kindness
only meaningless gestures
but whom, i gave, grieved for
years
he just didn't like me enough, they scolded me
or maybe
i didn't like myself enough
but he crept in
disturbed my rest
reminding me
of everything i thought was real, but was deceived
by my own sight
he was right
all the love in the world wasn't actually there
within me, for him
even though i loved him
as if it were

each moment that passes that i won't remember
each photo i capture to remember, but fail to record
will mean nothing
when i can't retain

my fundamental truth
within this broken moment,
and yet can still recall
the imaginary one
about a boy
who never
really
mattered

and so i claw my way through
this second go around
only for the darkness to carry me further
beneath the waters
for my shelter
now destroyed by time
i can barely see
as i keep dipping under
trying to catch a glimpse
of how i was better off
thinking
rather than knowing
i was drowning

i catch a glimpse of him
at the edge, the same edge
as he waits for me
to show up
everyday, every hour
hoping beyond hope
knowing
there is now a height
a mountain

that i can't overcome
and yet, he waits
patiently
searching for me on that island
binoculars in hand, voice horse
while
my head lay back
in surrender
only white skies to question
if i had already
passed

it was death
its stance was like stone
it weighted me further down
no arms
to reach
no power
to kick
to ascend
to rise
to hope

i drift

chemical
hormonal
emotional
mental
robbed me of oxygen and
deprived me of sight
took

my dreams
my memory
my time
of that which i traded my soul for

of that which i traded for my son

i hate
i hate what wasn't mines
what is no longer mines
i hate being back
for no other reason
but to make sure this never happened again
as if the hate
was not a cover for the anger
the disappointment
the sadness
the defeat
the false celebration
of hope

quiet descends
as i hold my breath

this is where i am at
and
this
is
where
i will
end.

knockout

and just like that
back at the starting line
no longer forward
no turning back
but this time
there is no island
already soaked
already under
and then he asks me,
should i stay home today?

he is helpless in the recognition
he will be helpless in the final battle
it was truth
alone, is where i reside
confirmation
anticipation
of a self undone

it's no longer an invisible war
echoing in the dead of night
floundering in the middle of my sentences
i am bleeding out
and all i do is gasp
for air
and he thinks
this is just me making conversation

i tell no one
i will die in this
turns out a truth that will never be believed
this will take me one day

because i know
everything i think
everything i feel
is
not
true
just a hallucination
of every fear
of every disappointment
of every shortcoming
i wasn't able to burn

so,
i stand still
i let it cut me
i let it scar me
i let it scare me
i let it change me
forever
and my greatest sword is stillness
so i let it destroy me
rain on me until i am pounded to the ground
with no more space on my skin
to be harmed
in hopes
it does not kill me
in hopes
it does not reach my heart
in hopes
that it thinks i am already dead
and retreats

my skin is threadbare
my will too
in the end
i will have destroyed
my life
some parts
most parts
that which are not already gone

i stand in my truth
a fiction
only for me
a mirage
only for him
my mind has gone just out of my reach
and he asks me again,
should i stay?

these are your limitations
your inability to recognize
that
death sits with me
like a patient companion

leave. stay. just go.
isn't it all the same when he is not really here
when he doesn't really see
what is in front of him
when he can't
recognize
there is nothing left
to fight for

when there is no one left
to fight for

it is a knockout

raise the white flag

i
am
surrendering.

roulette

the ceiling drops
and there is no where for me to go
but down

rise up
rise up
go
as if a battle cry could change the circumstances
to my mental collapse
trust me
if only i could go somewhere else besides
here

i float each day
waiting for the shadows
when no one wants anything from me
when i can grieve without interruptions
when i can attempt to numb without witnesses
help comes in words
that aren't backed up by knowledge
and all there is left is
silence

it's how i prefer it
blindness
i hear nothing but my emptiness
proving to me the one thing i know for sure
that no one can believe
i now have proof

i have been drained
devoid of my powers

and lost in my ability to do nothing
when the tides come
and take me out each night
on cue
like the familiar song
but with a surprise ending
a game of roulette
to carry you out and under
once more,
perhaps
only once more
waiting
for the water to fill your ears
fill your throat
with something, anything
in hopes
you'd forget you wanted to
resurface

its brighter here than i imagined
there is a sound past quiet
only i hear

i descend
despite
knowing

rise up
rise
come up
or float up.

we went to the mountains

and we went to the mountains
to be at the same place, but with a different door
bigger windows
to gaze out of
to become
still
with the trees to shield us from
final separation
we emptied the trash
turned off the heat
and packed what we remembered
exhausted
knowing we forgot most
of what we wanted to keep
with
us
all these years

it was clique to escape here
almost futile to suggest
god would meet us in
a place where
here
and there
are the same
the winding roads
take us above the clouds
in the fog
struggling to find a spot in the distance
so i don't loose
my place
so i don't loose

where we are
and where we always wanted to go
slow, slow down
i urge
don't rush
i want to make it
i want to see
what is beyond the clouds
beyond the fog
beyond what i can see
we are not lost
we are simply
in this place,
in
not yet out

so sit
take a seat
there is an emptiness besides me
that only he can fill
that i asked him to have
i promised to keep
for him
and only him
why won't he just sit
down
with me
in a stranger's house
in our distress
when the waters
are drowning me
why won't he sit

does he no longer hear me
can he no longer hear
is he immersed in fear
or do i no longer have a voice
instead he brushes off
my sputtering tears
that land
on
the
back
of
his neck

and i have to remind him
say it twice, the same
four times, differently
see me
see me
see
me
see
i am waiting for him to show up
i am waiting for him
so i can stop waiting
to feel
like something other than someone's wife
someone's mother
i do not want to be completed by
someone else's sentence
that privilege i own
i create
this is not his

and for the fifth time i say
see
i do not want to wait for him
but the promise was, to wait
in case
he
got
lost

and he turns to me
as he always does
my face, surprises him
i am not filled with his fears
i am only filled with
the desire
to be more
feel more
be touched more
by something other than
darkness
these days turned into years
silences turned into contempt
love turned
backwards, forwards, over and over
so smooth
it slips through our fingers
with nothing to hold onto
but a breath
caught up between
gasping for air
and monologuing
to be right

i am devastated
abandoned within
this isolation from where i belong in the world
it lifts silently out of me
the breath that is rightfully mines
that i was born with
that i
keep
for myself
tucked between my sleeve and my wrist
in case
just in case
god had mercy on me
and this hope
this wish
this dream
this impossibility
can try
to be
again

meanwhile i carry it everywhere i go
every time i stand, i feel it there
every time i sit, it peeks out
every time i cry, its weight doubles
i feel it
as if it too abandoned me
trying to figure out where i went wrong
what i did not live up to
what i sold myself as
trying to find a reason
why the world

shouldn't give up
on what i am capable of being
a dirty secret my past is aware of
and all those who left
join in
the chorus
reminding me
to let
it
and them
finally
go

but its still there
in between my wrist
and a sleeve that now is too short
to hide
my longing

but it is
his unawareness
to
what he
comes home to
who tucks in our son
who traded herself
for a dream that betrayed
and gives up each day
after he has fallen asleep
during my
mid-sentence

silences me
knowing
realizing
he too,
has left

my friend
my lover
my person
he is not here anymore
he has forgotten
that there is someone
that misses him when he leaves
when he falls away
into the waters
when he forgets
he has a boat, with us
with you
i see
hiding, cowering,
broken
heart torn by a past that seems to be unable to be undone
by a self not fully formed
not given a chance
to see light
to see his light
i holler
but he is already below
his hearing gone
his gaze floating to the sky
to the invisible force that greets him in this moment
that makes him feel

the holiness skipped him

the warning was and still is
we are disappearing
fading
into this platitude
of disgruntled spouses
separated by
ancient roles
we must fill
because society can't imagine
something more
because we can't figure out how to do
something else
we are lost
suffocated by responsibilities to uphold
something we have never valued
something we have never wanted
how
did
we
get
so far
here

is this where we end
lost in the fog
suffocated by our own wounds
that we can't heal
is this where
on the road
to a place

we can't imagine
we can't dream of
but beholden to a fog we can't see through
we can't trust through

so i say once more,
through the fog
no where near the heavens
but higher than we've been before
why can't he see

why
can't
i

so i will share with him what to do
as his lover
not his mother
sit
hold my hand
look into my eyes
remind me
of who you once were
still are
promised to be
you did not lie
you did not betray
you stopped
showing up
thinking your shadow
would be enough
would fool us enough

you thought
this could be enough

and i will remind him
like i remind myself:

i am
whole
i am enough
and i deserve more
from myself
to show up
to follow up
to stand up
to all the demons
and believe
in something more
in my existence
in my purpose
in my ability
to wake and rise again tomorrow

this
i share with him
my battle cry
my own song
so that he
will find his song with his words
and
sing it
so loud
i

will have it memorized

you are my love
you are on purpose
we are on purpose
and as i am discovering
i too
am
on purpose
everything that has happened
everything that is happening
and where you collapse
and where you rise
is
where
you will soar

if only he could meet me here
if he could
arrive
with his own words
his own hymn

himself

you

i promise
we won't have to go anywhere
to go
to the mountains...

...so for the last time
and the first time
i say

see me

but now
i see
what i couldn't before

myself.

it all went fine

i think why not me
why wasn't it simple
straightforward
painless
joyful
why wasn't it more than it was
or even less

i am not jealous
i am glad she does not know of this
that she won't carry
for years
like i know
it changes
how i see
and what i missed

i sense my own
resentment
in the back of my throat
hiding behind my words
burning
filling my eyes
with all the emotion
as if
the past could have been different
as if it was possible
to forgive
that invisible reason
that did this to me

i ask

why
why was it so different
so painful
so long
so
unforgettable
when i could have had
a more meaningless
moment

i want to rid myself of this
knowledge
i don't want to have to process it
to forgive what wasn't
and to find
the light
in what was
pitch. black. darkness.
i want to rewrite
all that was written for me
find the words to heal
the unseen
change my story
without changing
you

i want
those two years back
filled with memories
i could remember
that i filled with
my love

my joy
not
the sting of seawater in my mouth
up my nose
the panic and terror
of drowning each day
figuring out
how to leave
without abandoning
wondering
when
it is time

but i didn't drown
i'm on the other side
as if
i never suffered
as if
i can remember
as if
i could feel your love
as if
i didn't want the waves to cover me
and
end it all

but it was
it happened
it is mines
the point of no return
when it becomes yours
you just can't see

the worst happened
to you
and no one
will ever remember
or understand
all that was lost
like a natural disaster
it too,
will change the course
and never let one return
home

so tell me
how do i move on
and find the reason
to let go
of what has happened
to me
and my story
and fall in love
with pieces
that i hobbled together
to make sense
to make beautiful again
with words
no one can understand
but feel

take it
take it from me
take it
and change it

alkalize it
because
i can't
i can't open my eyes
i can't stop seeing scars
i can't do this
alone

it went fine, she said.

and i remind myself
it can
still
be

someday.

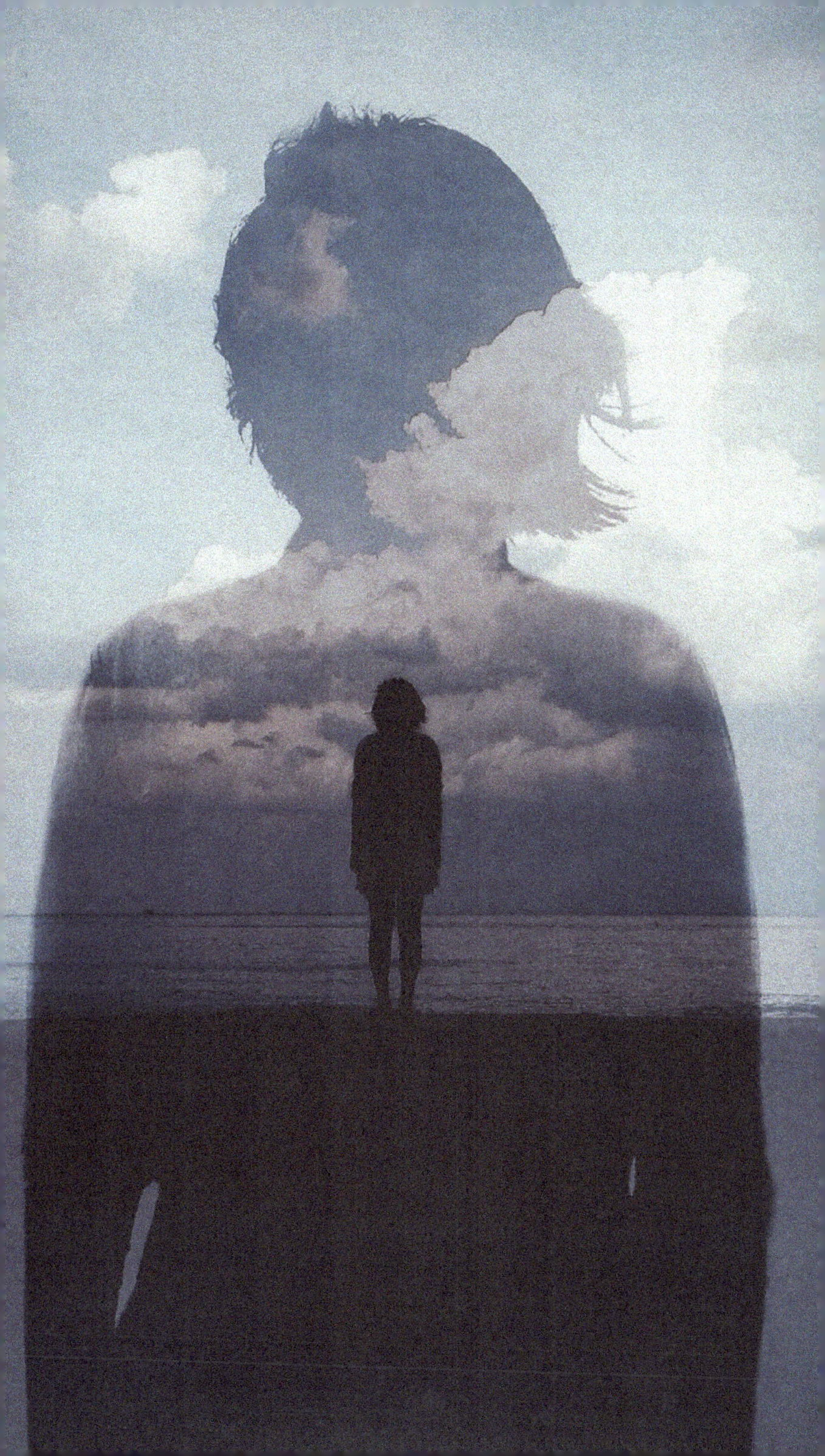

birth marks

*After two and a half years,
it was finally over.*

its over
days, weeks, months
years
and it has ended

my eyes strain at the sun
as i pick myself up and look
around
my heart collapses
everything
is
broken

what do i take
what do i leave
when it all meant so much
when it all means
too much
my heart
grieves for its body
all the work
struggle to become whole
to become me
to become more
i became less

pounded down to a grain of sand
i stand on the mainland
standing amongst grains
looking out into the ocean
and i can't see
where i was

where i've been
but my scars tell me
what i survived
i imagine
what he was looking out at
when there is nothing to see from here
nothing
to focus on
could he see me
or was
it just hope
that i was out there
was he talking to me
or was he
asking
god
to bring me back

his hand slips quietly in mines
my head turns
shame colors his face for
he could not do more
did not know how
and yet, proud
i did not do more
relieved
i did not find out how
grateful
i did not
let go

i am on the other side

it is as i remembered
nothing has changed
but everything and anything within
was destroyed
inhaled into circumstances
fractured like dried paint
pieces that can never
be restored
to it's original state of birth
scars litter my skin
as if a map
to my collapse
proof of a volcanic disruption
of soul
now birth marks
of another kind

his hand
familiar and warm
like the day he slipped me that token
i didn't need
to get home
the token
he needed
to hold my hand
to remind me
i am not
alone
and can not be defined
by the bad things that have happened to me
or what loss had
ensued

small arms wrap around my leg
tiny fingers press into my scars
mama
i look down to see my eyes greet me
you are the child i never was
the joy i didn't have
the love i never knew i was capable of
you cradle my heart, fiercely
until i can find my place
on the sand
among the grains
in the light
on the shores

i am home
i can feel the sun
i can feel my son

the end
the beginning

the birth
my rebirth.

emancipation

i fill my lungs
with a relief that washes over me
like my own tears
my own
sorrow
flowing from my head
around the curve of my eyelid
to the tip of my chin
free falling to the ground
finally
completely
out of my heart
off of my soul
shattered
on the uneven payment
below

there is a contrast
a dividing line i see behind me
of where i was
and where i am
of where i wanted to be
and where i strive towards
two completely different places
phases
of being
broken open
by the weight of
a transformation
that took four years
an alchemy
that took forty

i am no longer
at the mercy of the child within
i am now the cornerstone
of the woman
who can tell that child to rest
to cease her worries
about where she goes, how she will get there
and what she will do
so that she can
embrace what she does not know
knowing she will have learned all that she needs
in the moment she needs
embrace who she is, who she is not,
and how wonderful both are

she will
dive hands first through the forest
muddied palms, calloused knees
open her eyes under the beating waves
clouded vision, shortened breaths
lock on brilliant blue sky as she falls
arms outstretched, floor removed
and say no
kindly, respectfully, purposefully
so that she can
hold space
hold time
hold
so that she can finish
grieving

so let the tears fall

let the sky cloud over
i know where the sun is at
i know the east
is where i will rise
and where
i will find my moon
in the darkest
of days
in the middle of my nightmares
should the land
retreat
beneath the ocean's waves again
i know
where my breath begins
and trust that
where it ends
will not be my downfall
will not be my mistake
will
in fact
be
my saving grace.

these things i carry

and so i ask
what was all this for
the darkness
why was i to be
mutilated at birth
joy mangled in a
reflection unrecognizable
voice stolen by a storm louder than i could scream
self
discarded by the undertow
how do i piece together all that i once wanted to become
into someone
greater
than that i could have ever imagined

how

and i stand in stillness
at the starting line
everyone has already left
now, within the climax of their finish line
i lean down
and touch the floor
with a grace i hadn't known before
on my knees
the scars press, not yet healed
marking where i almost drowned
where i lost my breath
how far i've gone
how long it's been
no one is watching
no one is left to

witness
this time
but for the first time
when
where
and how far
i'll fly

the cheers rise from within
louder than the downpour
drowning out the echoes of my anxious breath
the empty stadium
bringing the ocean to my eyes
instead of my feet
lifting my chin
my heart
towards the sun

where have you been all this time
i've been waiting for you

i remain suspended in thought
in the joy of knowing
the trauma of my imperfections
did not
steal my purpose
did not handicap my hope
did not
let me
fall
asleep under the tides

so, release me from the strings
that play each time the wind blows
and gather me close to the reasons
i've discovered to be greater than
myself
head bowed
knowing how far
down
i had to rise to make it back
the pain that falls on the back of my pressed hands
comfort me knowing
this too shall pass

for it has passed
and
i
did not

the clouds part
and there is an opening
i see
and i let the winds
uplift me
and these things i carry
invisible and permanent
to fly
with me

it's time
it's time to soar

I will soar once again.

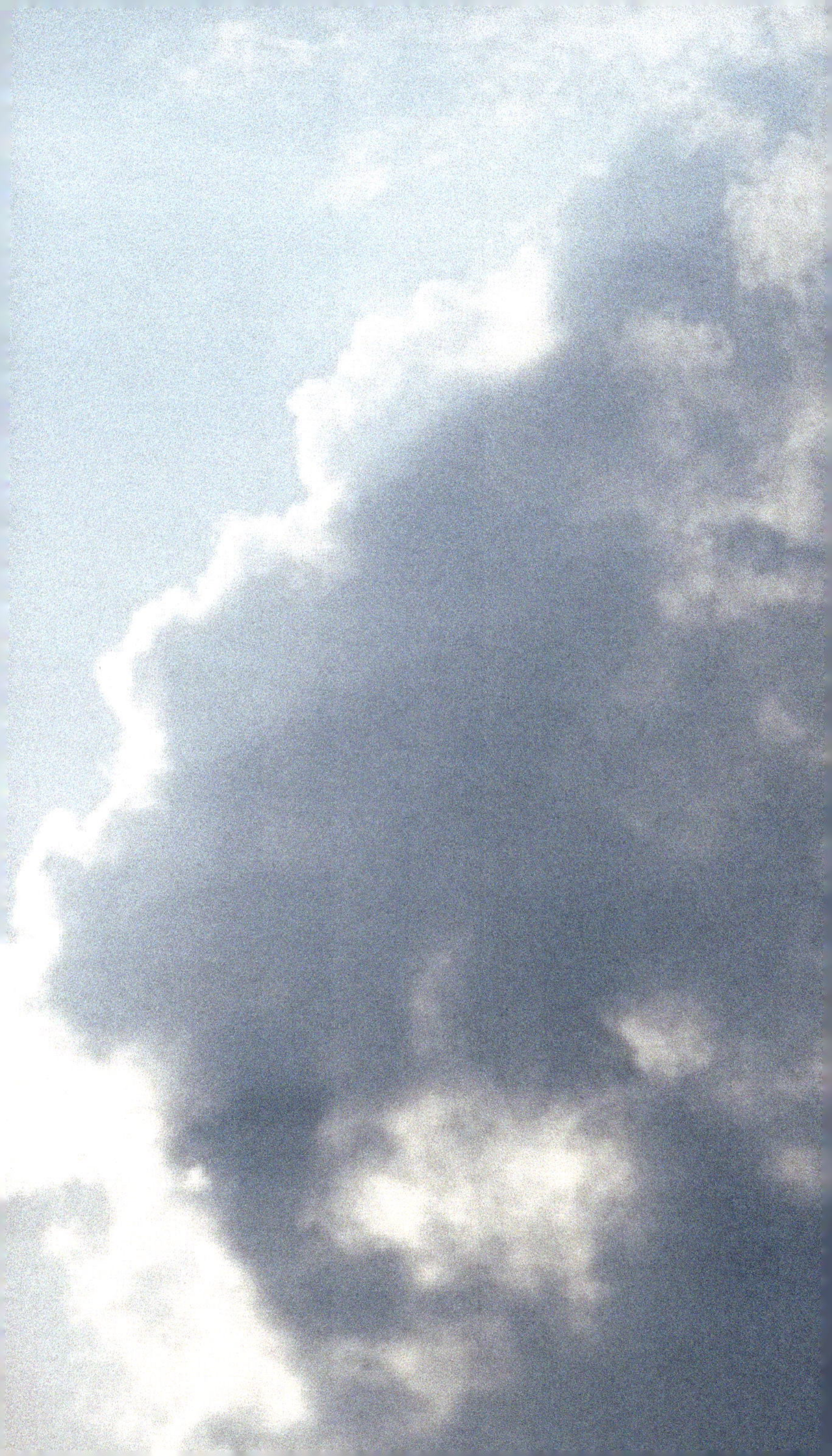

AFTERWORD

My son is now six. He runs as fast as the wind, takes a dramatic sigh when I ask him to do something he doesn't want to, links his arm around my neck in the few minutes each morning before he gets up for the day, and smiles at me with the same eyes. I see myself. I see my husband.

And finally, I see my son.

So much has changed and yet, all that has happened does not leave me. I walk with it when I watch with envy as new-mothers crowd the playground with their smiles gently camouflaging their post birth struggles. When my son walks over to me when I've had a hard day, he recognizes my sadness like my husband does. And when I confess to a new mother I am trying to connect with, with honesty, brevity, and calm, that I had PPD, the relief on their faces merge mines, as they share with me similar journeys of strength, trial and the destruction left by their storms. Scars hidden behind the rehearsed story.

Turns out we are not alone.

For those in the midst of their storms: Help through this will come in many different forms. Find the avenues that work for you. Remember this as you move through this and past this:

You are not alone. We are all waves in same ocean. We must remember, even though we do not know each other, our arms are linked. We are linked. I see you.

And through this book, I know you see me. Through my words, I hope you find something you didn't know you were looking for. It is okay to feel devastated. It is okay to struggle. It is okay that it takes time, maybe years, for this to pass. And it is okay, to not be okay.

Or ever again, the same.

Everything eventually changes. The one constant in life. I leaned on this in all those moments, I cried to myself in the corner of the kitchen hidden from my son as he watched TV. When the biggest win of the day was that I did not walk into the ocean. And as I comforted myself, after those who could not stand with me, faded into the background.

Five years later and it is done. It is over.

And from the rain, poured these words. From the storm, left scars of a different color. This book is my trail of breadcrumbs, where I can see where I was, where I traveled through and how I made it home.

To my therapists: I am grateful for your your kindness, your compassion, your sliding scale, and your steadfast belief that I would eventually rise again. Thank you for your voice in the dark and in the silence.

To my husband: Thank you for looking for me in the ocean, even when you saw nothing. You showed up believing that I will too, again, someday. And in those moments I would go under, I knew you were searching. You never gave up. Even when I tried to convince you otherwise.

To my son: You are the most beautiful gift I have ever been given. You have changed me completely and have gifted me the privilege of becoming a mother and knowing a love, I had never known. I share these things I carry, knowing, this moment in my journey does not define me, you, or our time together here on earth. I love you, to another galaxy and back, forever and ever.

Theresa

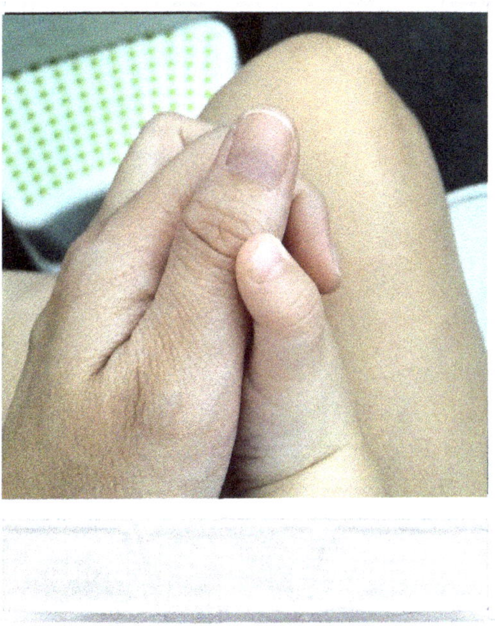

ABOUT THE AUTHOR

Theresa Wu is a filmmaker, screenwriter and poet. Daughter of immigrants from Hong Kong, Theresa's artistic works explores the rich complexities of Asian American lives within America as well as deeply personal experiences as a woman, mother and artist.

Theresa is an award winning filmmaker who completed her MFA in Directing at Columbia University and her BA in Film at the Pennsylvania State University. Her short film, *Smoke and Mirrors,* went on to win the Director's Guild of America's Best Student Filmmaker Award (Asian American/East Coast), the CINE Golden Eagle Award and the Silver at the CA Film Festival. Her films have also screened in NYC, LA, Washington DC and Philadelphia at numerous film festivals.

She firmly believes that her artistic work is enriched by work with at-risk and under-served populations. For over 8 years, she has served in a variety of roles as Creative Director, Teaching Artist and/or Mentor to homeless youth, emancipated foster youth, and seniors to arm them with the skills, tools and platform to showcase their voices through writing, poetry, film and storytelling in both NYC and LA.

For more information about Theresa Wu or her artistic works, please visit www.kowancreative.com

Milton Keynes UK
Ingram Content Group UK Ltd.
UKHW050411180524
442738UK00008B/54